Motoring Memories

Compiled by Robert Grieves

© Robert Grieves 1988

ISBN 0 9506381 2 9

Cover design by Isaac McCaig

Published by
XS Publications
9 Pearson Drive
Renfrew, PA4 0BD
041-886 2562

Printed by
Cordfall Ltd.
041-332 4640

A 'run down' in the country.
Many of the firms producing picture post cards in Edwardian days issued sets with a motoring theme and not all of them were complimentary. There was still an anti-automobile feeling among certain sections of the community which did not disappear until the advent of the 1914–18 War. Shown here is a typical example of this kind of card and below we see a road sign of the same period aimed principally at the type of motorist depicted above.

TO MOTORISTS.

Please DRIVE SLOWLY so as not to SMOTHER the growing Crops with DUST.

INTRODUCTION

More than any other inanimate object, we hold our cars in the highest regard. The family car has in fact become a member of the family. If for any reason it is not immediately available to us, then we tend to miss its presence as we would that of an absent friend.

Indeed it has been whispered that some men think more of their cars than they do their wives . . . There is also a school of thought that cars, like pets, have personalities and even develop the eccentricities of their owners.

Be all this as it may, the car has certainly become an integral part of our everyday lives and increasingly more so as the years progress.

There are few car owners who do not reminisce as they remember with affection their first set of wheels — their 1947 Minx, 1953 Consul or some seniors may even recall their 1926 Bullnose or the like. This little book is dedicated to such people. Unashamedly nostalgic, it will transport the reader back in time to a more leisurely age when motoring must indeed have been a joy.

I have spanned approximately the first 50 years of this century. Admittedly, to most of us the earliest cars pictured will mean no more than a name we have either read about or heard our grandfathers mention. Some, such as the famous Scottish three A's — Albion, Argyll and Arrol Johnston will be more familiar, even although we may not remember them. Incidentally, our excellent Transport Museum in Glasgow has examples of all three.

This, however, is not a volume confined to Scottish built cars (which would admittedly justify a book on its own); rather it is a tour around Scotland showing glimpses of our motoring past.

Positive identification of some of the cars is difficult. Rather than commit an error to print, if there is any doubt as to the make of a vehicle, then I have either purposefully not named it or at least indicated my uncertainty in the accompanying caption. In this connection I would be delighted to hear from anyone who can accurately name any of the unspecified makes or perhaps rectify any unwitting errors which may have crept in.

Most boys of my own age group recognised cars by their distinctive radiators. There were still plenty of these around when we went to school in the 1950s. Quite frankly I would have difficulty in identifying many of their present day counterparts.

I have also included a section on public transport as the motorbus was really the people's car before car ownership came into its own. Often the only opportunity many folk had to visit the coast or country was by charabanc. In the early years of motoring only the more affluent members of a community could afford to own an automobile, such as the laird at the local big house or the village doctor. Consequently people were much more dependent on the bus than nowadays.

The most modern views are from the 1950's, the decade when cars started to become mundane monsters of the motorways, losing much of the charm and individuality enjoyed by their predecessors.

Although I have not set out to provide a complete coverage of motoring matters, I trust that most readers will learn something from the book. Who knows, you may see one of your own former cars among the illustrations and at the very least you ought to recognise some of the locations, albeit perhaps somewhat changed today.

I hope *Motoring Memories* will be enjoyed as much as I have enjoyed compiling it.

Robert Grieves

9 Pearson Drive,
RENFREW

ORIGINAL ALLOCATION LIST OF MOTOR INDEXATION

IDENTIFICATION MARKS

SCOTLAND: COUNTIES

Aberdeenshire	SA	Fifeshire	SP	Nairnshire	AS
Argyllshire	SB	Forfarshire	SR	Orkney	BS
Ayrshire	SD	Haddingtonshire	SS	Peeblesshire	DS
Banffshire	SE	Inverness-shire	ST	Perthshire	ES
Berwickshire	SH	Kincardineshire	SU	Renfrewshire	HS
Buteshire	SJ	Kinross-shire	SV	Ross and Cromarty	JS
Caithness-shire	SK	Kirkcudbrightshire	SW	Roxburghshire	KS
Clackmannanshire	SL	Lanarkshire	V	Selkirkshire	LS
Dumfriesshire	SM	Linlithgowshire	SX	Stirlingshire	MS
Dumbartonshire	SN	Midlothian		Sutherlandshire	NS
Elginshire	SO	(Edinburghshire)	SY	Wigtownshire	OS
				Zetland	PS

SCOTLAND: BOROUGHS

Aberdeen	RS	Glasgow	G	Leith	WS
Dundee	TS	Govan	US	Paisley	XS
Edinburgh	S	Greenock	VS	Partick	YS

ENGLAND & WALES: COUNTIES

Anglesey	EY	Ely, Isle of	EB	London	A	Southampton	AA
Bedfordshire	BM	Essex	F	Merionethshire	FF	Staffordshire	E
Berkshire	BL	Flintshire	DM	Middlesex	H	Suffolk, East	BJ
Breconshire	EU	Glamorganshire	L	Monmouthshire	AX	Suffolk, West	CF
Buckinghamshire	BH	Gloucestershire	AD	Montgomeryshire	EP	Surrey	P
Cambridgeshire	CE	Herefordshire	CJ	Norfolk	AH	Sussex, East	AP
Cardiganshire	EJ	Hertfordshire	AR	Northamptonshire	BD	Sussex, West	BP
Carmarthenshire	BX	Huntingdonshire	EW	Northumberland	X	Warwickshire	AC
Carnarvonshire	CC	Kent	D	Nottinghamshire	AL	Westmorland	EC
Cheshire	M	Lancashire	B	Oxfordshire	BW	Wight, Isle of	DL
Cornwall	AF	Leicestershire	AY	Pembrokeshire	DE	Wiltshire	AM
Cumberland	AO	Lincolnshire,		Peterborough,		Worcestershire	AB
Denbighshire	CA	parts of Holland	DO	Soke of	FL	Yorkshire	
Derbyshire	R	Lincolnshire, parts of		Radnorshire	FO	(East Riding)	BT
Devonshire	T	Kesteven	CT	Rutland	FP	Yorkshire	
Dorset	BF	Lincolnshire,		Salop	AW	(North Riding)	AJ
Durham	J	parts of Lindsey	BE	Somerset	Y	Yorkshire	
						(West Riding)	C

ENGLAND & WALES: BOROUGHS

Barrow-in-Furness	EO	Coventry	DU	Lincoln	FE	Rotherham	ET
Bath	FB	Croydon	BY	Liverpool	K	St. Helens	DJ
Birkenhead	CM	Derby	CH	Manchester	N	Salford	BA
Birmingham	O	Devonport	DR	Middlesbrough	DC	Sheffield	W
Blackburn	CB	Dudley	FD	Newcastle-upon-Tyne		Southampton	CR
Bolton	BN	Exeter	FJ		BB	South Shields	CU
Bootle	EM	Gateshead	CN	Newport		Stockport	DB
Bournemouth	EL	Gloucester	FH	(Monmouth)	DW	Sunderland	BR
Bradford		Great Yarmouth	EX	Northampton	DF	Swansea	CY
(Yorkshire)	AK	Grimsby	EE	Norwich	CL	Walsall	DH
Brighton	CD	Halifax	CP	Nottingham	AU	Warrington	ED
Bristol	AE	Hanley	EH	Oldham	BU	West Bromwich	EA
Burnley	CW	Hastings	DY	Oxford	FC	West Ham	AN
Burton-upon-Trent	FA	Huddersfield	CX	Plymouth	CO	West Hartlepool	EF
Bury	EN	Ipswich	DX	Portsmouth	BK	Wigan	EK
Canterbury	FN	Kingston-upon-Hull	AT	Preston	CK	Wolverhampton	DA
Cardiff	BO	Leeds	U	Reading	DP	Worcester	FK
Chester	FM	Leicester	BC	Rochdale	DK	York	DN

The former Scottish County boundaries appropriate throughout the period covered by *Motoring Memories*

Shetland

Orkney

Lewis

Harris

Caithness

Sutherland

Ross and Cromarty

Moray

Nairn

Banff

Aberdeen

Inverness

Kincardine

Angus

Perth

Argyll

Clackmannan

Kinross

Fife

Dunbarton

Stirling

West Lothian

East Lothian

Renfrew

Midlothian

Berwick

Bute

Lanark

Peebles

Selkirk

Ayr

Roxburgh

Dumfries

Kirkcudbright

Wigtown

England

Motoring Infancy

fig. 1. An M.M.C. car of 1900 built by the Motor Manufacturing Company at Coventry but assembled along with others by John Love of Kirkcaldy (who is driving), one of Scotland's pioneer motorists. Note that this car, and some of the others in these earliest illustrations, bears no registration number. Licensing did not commence until late 1903 and by 1904 most areas were issuing their own index letters.

fig. 2. Turn of the century motoring alongside the River Tweed between Peebles and Innerleithen with some of the local pioneer automobilists, to give them the grand title often used at that time. Left to right are Mr Ernest Thiem on a De Dion motor tricycle towing a wicker trailer; Mr G. Bridges with a Locomobile steam car (note tiller steering); Mr Laurence Bell with his home assembled car, and Mr James Shiell on a De Dion tricycle similar to that on the left but without a trailer.

fig. 3. The interior of John Stirling's motor works at Granton, Edinburgh about 1902. This factory had previously been used until 1900 by William Peck to build his Madelvic electric broughams, one of which may just be seen on the left. The two seater car may have been an early Stirling. Scotland's first motor car showroom was opened in 1899 by Stirling in Sauchiehall Street, Glasgow.

fig. 4. A fine atmospheric scene in Shore Street, Kirkwall in early Edwardian days showing the first car to visit Orkney, a Daimler of around 1898 brought by a holidaymaker. The throng of small boys running after it shows just how great a novelty the occasion was. Similar scenes could have been witnessed throughout the country at that time, when motor vehicles were in their infancy and merited great attention.

fig. 5. An American built Locomobile steam car at John O'Groat's in 1900 driven by Hubert W. Egerton prior to leaving for Land's End. (The first end to end car run had been made three years earlier in a Daimler by Henry Sturmey, first editor of the Autocar.) Driving the Locomobile was a very wearisome business as the steamer required constant attention during the journey, consuming 26 gallons of water every 20 miles.

MOTORING IN
GLEN COE
1902
———

This motor car probably the first to drive through Scotland's most famous glen was preceded by a cyclist who warned the villagers that a motor car was on the way from Bridge of Orchy and to keep a look out in case of accidents!
———

fig. 6. This scene proves that one should not automatically assume what is printed to be always correct. The Edwardian picture post card is captioned 'Motoring in Glencoe, 1902', which cannot be the case as the Albion car was registered in Renfrewshire HS 9 and since licensing did not get under way until 1904 the date is obviously wrong. The so-called Red Flag Act which had limited speed to 4 m.p.h. and required someone to precede the vehicle had been repealed in 1896.

fig. 7.   Identification of Edwardian cars is often difficult owing to the visual similarity of many different types. This scene in Stirling Street, Denny, around 1902 shows what is believed may be a French built Hurtu. Its four occupants are well clad to face the elements. Note the sprag which prevents rolling backwards is trailing below the car.

fig. 8.   An example of the popular French built De Dion Bouton car seen outside Inverbeg Hotel on Loch Lomondside in 1904. Judging by the pipers in this view, SN 20 could have had a Highland welcome when it pulled up for refreshments.

9

fig. 9 The Caledonian Motor Car Co. Ltd. of Union Street, Aberdeen built cars under the name Caledonian in early Edwardian years and was also the local agent for the French Peugeot company. This view shows the Edwardian elegance of 1904 Peugeot RS 5 sporting a fine pair of acetylene headlamps. The leather -clad chauffeur has his uniform complemented with gaiters and he is thus ready to cope with the vagaries of the weather in this completely open model. Covered saloon cars remained in the minority until the late 1920s.

fig. 10. (Top, opposite) The lady occupants of this similar Peugeot were also suitably dressed to face the Scottish climate, albeit more fashionably so. The Edinburgh number S 10 dates this car as registered in December 1903, when motor licensing started there. Many owners transferred their numbers to later cars, proving that 'cherished numbers' have been with us since the early days, often confusing motoring historians.

fig. 11. (Below, opposite) Market Place, North Berwick in 1904 with George Fowler, proprietor of the local motor and posting establishment in the rear seat of his Bridgeton built 10/12 H.P. Argyll hire car, with East Lothian registration number SS 36. Note the advert on the wall offering dog carts, brakes and victorias for hire, these all horse-drawn of course.

11

fig. 12. The pony pulling the governess cart on the left does not deign to look at its new noisy rival which was in fact TS1, the first privately registered car in Dundee, a De Dion of 1903 owned by a Mr Alexander Watt. For a lady to drive an automobile in those days was considered extremely daring, almost to the point of being 'fast', especially without a male escort.

fig. 13. The make of SU 79 was probably Renault, registered in Kincardineshire in 1904 and possibly with its home in Johnshaven where this view was taken. The inevitable crowd of small boys has gathered round to stare at the new-fangled machine.

fig. 14. These four intrepid gentlemen are seated aboard a 1904 White steam car, imported from the White Sewing Machine Company, Cleveland, Ohio. It had a compound engine which could run for 100 miles on one tankful of water and its makers proclaimed that 'its operating parts are so arranged that a lady need have no fear of soiling even a glove in running the car.' Despite the London number this car was owned by a family in West Lothian.

fig. 15. Another of the many French manufactured imports was the De Dietrich. This example was registered in Midlothian with the SY index mark. The occupants appear to be an elderly gentleman of means and his chauffeur, not forgetting Fido on the running board.

13

Motor Meets

Motor Meet at Philiphaugh.

fig. 16. Philiphaugh House near Selkirk (now demolished) was the setting in 1904 for this view of Scotland's first major motor meet. Here we see examples of many early Edwardian automobiles including Albion, Cadillac, Daimler, De Dion, Mercedes, Panhard, Peugeot, Renault and Rover. In the foreground with registration LS3 is an Arrol Johnston dogcart occupied by the Strang-Steele family, owners of Philiphaugh. In the centre of the photo is a Wolseley registered G 1 and driven by R.J. Smith, then secretary of the Scottish Automobile Club. (Compare this with Fig. 23 which again shows G 1 but on a later car, which was an early example of a number being transferred to a subsequent vehicle.)

fig. 17. A fine parade of Edwardian cars in the grounds of imposing Hopetoun House, South Queensferry. Leading is a Peugeot registered S6 followed by a Daimler bearing the coveted S1 registration and transferred to this car from his original Delahaye by Sir John Macdonald, one time Lord Justice-Clerk and first president of the Scottish Automobile Club. Also visible are S 559, an Argyll; Y 324, a Daimler and SY 84, a De Dion.

fig. 18. Edwardian motorists and their friends would often meet and drive off together in their cars for the day. This seems to have been one such occasion, with a quartette of Edinburgh registered machines. From the left are Argyll S 559 (also in the scene above); Peugeot S 585; unidentified S 685 and Wolseley-Siddeley S 898 about to leave from what is believed to be the Grange area of the city.

Edwardian Rallying

Motor sport was just as popular in the early days as it is now as may be seen from these Edwardian scenes of Scottish Automobile Club Reliability Trials, which commenced in 1905. The following views were taken on the taxing section which included the 'Rest and be Thankful' hill climb through Glen Croe. The present highway up the 'Rest' was opened in 1945 but the old road is still occasionally used for motor trials.

fig. 19. A view at the starting line in Glen Croe on the first day of the 1907 Scottish reliability trial. A group of well-dressed spectators watches as XS 53, an Arrol Johnston, prepares for the off. This was a 38-45 H.P. model entered by the New Arrol Johnston Car Company of Paisley. Just visible behind is an American 30 H.P. White steam car followed by a 40 H.P. French Berliet.

fig. 20. XS 60, a smaller 16-25 H.P. Arrol Johnston approaches the check point at the top of the 'Rest and be Thankful', also on the first day of the same trial, 25th June 1907. This too was a works-entered car from Paisley. In the background can be seen the ribbon of road winding up through Glen Croe.

fig. 21. One can almost smell the exhaust as this Humber, another entrant in the 1907 trial negotiates a hairpin bend towards the summit of 'the Rest'. The loose road surface was fairly typical of many of our highways at that time resulting as we see in a dust storm as each car passed. *17*

fig. 22. Under starter's orders at a hill climb from Lanark is DS 38, an Albion 12H.P. car registered in Peeblesshire in 1904. The driver was Mr Laurence Bell founder of the Peebles Motor Company and agent for Albion cars, and the starter was Mr T. Blackwood Murray, managing director of the Albion Motor Car Company.

fig. 23. G1 was a Wolseley-Siddeley owned by R. J. Smith, a founder member and former secretary of the R.S.A.C. It is seen here driven by 'R.J.' himself on an early competition run, probably in 1908, near Tummel Bridge in Perthshire. Compare this car with R. J. Smith's original Wolseley G1 in Fig. 16.

fig. 24   A scene on a stage during the 1909 Scottish Automobile Club reliability trial setting off from Gairloch Hotel, Wester Ross. In the foreground is LB 8515, an Italian 20 H.P. Lancia followed by DU 678, a 15 H.P. Rover.

fig. 25.   DA 303, a Birmingham registered Sunbeam open tourer described in contemporary publicity as 'the new live axle 14-20 H.P. model.' It is seen here during the S.A.C. reliability trial of 1909 descending Cairnwell Pass on the Braemar — Blairgowrie road. The Summit of this pass at 2199 feet is the highest altitude of a main road in Great Britain.

fig. 26. What the motoring smart set were wearing in 1908 when this view was taken outside the Anchor Inn at Coldingham, Berwickshire. It shows S 1264 an Edinburgh registered 20 H.P. 6 cylinder Standard with the unmistakable humped radiator favoured by that marque. The coachwork is of the Roi des Belges tourer type.

fig. 27. Small boys with big collars watch a hunt meet about 1908 at Torphichen, West Lothian, while the cars which have brought along the county set attract equal attention. From the left these are SX 40, a locally registered Rover 8 H.P. then a Humber just visible then a Daimler and finally a covered Napier. The Daimler was particularly fashionable amongst the upper classes by virtue of its Royal patronage from King Edward VII.

fig. 28. Inside the Inverness garage of MacRae and Dick around 1908 with an Argyll taxi nearest the camera. This concern which had graduated from horse-drawn transport was probably the foremost car hire firm in the north often also providing the services of a chauffeur to prosperous families who rented a Highland home for a term during summer.

fig. 29. One of George Fowler's later hire cars (his first may be seen in fig. 11) was SS 238 a Wolseley-Siddeley landaulette pictured in North Berwick during the Coronation celebrations for King George V in 1910. Fowler built up a considerable fleet of cars and charabancs in the seaside town and for many years was the local B.M.C. agent.

Taxi!

fig. 30. If you hailed a Glasgow cab in Edwardian days this is how it may have looked. G 1561 was a Delaunay-Belleville owned by one of the city hiring companies of the time, probably Wylie and Lochhead, agents for the French manufacturer whose cars were reckoned to be among the world's best.

fig. 31. Each uniformed driver stands beside his car awaiting custom at the cab rank outside Largs railway station. This scene of about 1908 shows a Standard followed by two Albion taxis.

fig. 32.+ fig. 33. Two views of S 1951, the same 15 H.P.Straker Squire of 1911 in very different surroundings. The upper scene is in Fettercairn on the edge of the fertile Howe of the Mearns in Kincardineshire. The arch was erected to commemorate the visit of Queen Victoria and her consort Prince Albert in 1861. The location of the lower view is not certain but thought to be crossing a ford in the border country. Note how both the side and headlamps are covered for protection and to prevent tarnishing

Three 'A's

The three famous A's of Scottish Motor Manufacturing were the Argyll, Arrol Johnston and Albion, all built within a few miles of each other. Albion ceased building private cars as early as 1913, but continued to produce commercial vehicles, while the other two concerns both ceased business in the early 1930s after several troubled final years of production.

The new works, Alexandria, Argyll Motors Limited.

fig. 34. A contemporary picture post card of 1905 showing the final construction of the somewhat pretentious Argyll Motors Factory in Alexandria. Scaffolding is erected around the main doorway above which is the magnificent stone carving of a motor car still to be seen today although sadly the fine building is in jeopardy. The over-ambitious works was opened in 1906 but never achieved its full potential thus contributing to the company failure in 1914.

fig. 35. A group of late Edwardian Argyll cars driven by Scottish motor agents and their friends outside Tarbet Hotel on Loch Lomondside. In 1911 four-wheel brakes were introduced on Argylls, reputed to be the first motor manufacturer in the world to adopt them as standard. This was all the more remarkable considering that many cars were fitted only with rear wheel brakes until well into the 1920s.

fig. 36. Inside the finishing shop of the New Arrol Johnston Car Co. factory at Underwood, Paisley around 1910 with two 11.9 H.P. models and on the right a 15.9 H.P. model in their final stage before completion. As may be seen, these had Renault type bonnets with dashboard radiators. The firm moved to a new factory in Dumfries in 1913 and the Beardmore Co. took over the Paisley works.

fig. 37. An Albion 15 H.P. torpedo de-luxe model with Lanarkshire registration V 1520 dating from 1911 which was produced until 1913 when Albion ceased production of private cars at their Scotstoun factory to concentrate on the more successful commercial chassis. The driver in this view is H. E. Fulton an Albion director and brother of Norman Fulton who was joint founder of the company in 1899 along with T.Blackwood Murray (see fig. 22)

fig. 38. An evocative city scene in Glasgow around 1910 looking up Renfield Street from its junction with Gordon Street. The Delaunay-Belleville parked on the left is similar to that in fig. 30 while driving towards the camera is an Argyll. At first glance the registration number of this car appears to be G1 but close inspection reveals it to be GD 1, which was the first of a batch of trade plates issued to the Argyll Motor Co. for test and delivery purposes.

fig. 39. A fine line of quality Edwardian automobiles with chauffeurs awaiting their presumably equally aristocratic owners at the Fife Arms Hotel in Braemar on Royal Deeside. A Daimler landaulette is followed by a 16 H.P. Albion landaulette and a Belgian built Minerva open tourer.

fig. 40. From some of the best known Scottish cars, let us look at perhaps the least known. This was a 'one-off' assembled in 1910 by Orkney pioneer motorist and garage owner W. R. Tullock, who is seen on the right with his Kirkwall built car which he registered as a St. Magnus. It was a 12 H.P. two cylinder vehicle and locally numbered BS 97. The car on the left is an early Daimler.

Tullock's are still in business in Kirkwall today, priding themselves as owners of Orkney's oldest established garage.

fig. 41. Steam cars achieved a mild degree of success mainly in the years prior to World War I. This view shows an example of possibly the best known make — Stanley, imported from Massachusetts, U.S.A. CN 258 had actually been converted to a bus and was operated by French of Coldingham between that village and the nearest railhead at Reston where the photo was taken in 1910.

The Joys of Motoring . . .

We live in an age of change, but some things never change. Running out of petrol, punctures and problems below the bonnet have caused frustration since the earliest days of motoring and still do of course.

fig. 42. The Isle of Bute was home to this locally registered two seater 6 H.P. Siddeley of 1904. Daughter watches as daddy fills the tank with petrol from a two gallon can. Petrol pumps were not commonplace until the late 1920s and originally fuel was usually bought in cans at hardware stores or even chemist shops.

fig. 43. Father changes the wheel of his Argyll while mother and sons wait patiently in the car. This scene, taken in 1912, clearly shows the gear levers (both of them!), the hand brake outside the bodywork and the splendid coiled bulb horn.

fig. 44. Another Argyll giving cause for concern. The despondent driver is distinctly disgruntled as his buddy buries himself below the bonnet.

A.A. and M.U. Patrol Inspector.

There's nothing like motoring (when you get stuck)
For testing your temper, endurance and pluck.

fig. 45. The rhyme below this Edwardian post card sums up this section of the book quite neatly.   *29*

fig. 46. Incredible though it may seem now, many car owners in Edwardian days could not maintain or even drive their own vehicles, employing a chauffeur instead. In this view, taken on the main north road near Dalwhinnie, Inverness-shire, we see the owner with chauffeur posing alongside S 1079 a 1908 Coventry built Humber. Note the bunch of 'lucky' heather in the radiator.

fig. 47. This was taken later during the journey with owner leaning on the radiator and companion in the driving seat while the chauffeur attempts to solve the mystery of a mechanical failure on the Humber, proving that their heather did not achieve much luck.

fig. 48. Every motorist dreads an accident. This argument took place between FG 1674 a Bean charabanc of the General Motor Carrying Co., Kirkcaldy and SF 7194 an Edinburgh registered Hillman 14 saloon, in Glenfarg in 1927 when the Hillman was new and the Bean only one year old.

A.A. and M.U. Patrol

fig. 49. The ultimate indignity! However a car on the road is worth two in the ditch and so this 10 H.P. Singer of around 1924 is rescued by a horse somewhere in the border country.

31

'.. any colour provided it's black'

Motor Ascent of Ben Nevis (near the Red Burn)   Copyright

Descending Ben Nevis (4,000 feet)   Copyright

fig. 50 + fig. 51 The ascent and descent of Britain's highest mountain in a Model T Ford provided widespread publicity for that company. This feat up and down Ben Nevis (4406') was successfully accomplished in 1911 by Henry Alexander whose father owned Edinburgh's main Ford agency. Ford went on to build an incredible fifteen million model Ts.

32

fig. 52. This Berwickshire example of a Model T Ford was registered SH 476 in 1912 and was used as a hiring car by Alexander Wait of Chirnside (at the wheel.) It is seen on the historic Union Chain Bridge which carries a minor road across the River Tweed near Paxton. Built in 1820, this was the first suspension bridge in the United Kingdom.

fig. 53. Another Tin Lizzie, as the Model T was affectionately known. This one dates from around 1916 and was in the hiring fleet operated by Guy Brothers of Aberlady, East Lothian, some of whose employees are seen posing with various motoring accessories (and a bottle of whisky!) *33*

fig. 54. An animated view of Bridge Street, Dunfermline around 1911 with SP 1300, a Fife registered Rover 12 prominent. In 1913 the Dunfermline and District Tramways Co. laid their tracks and erected poles and overhead wires in this street, altering its appearance. Nowadays Bridge Street is one-way towards the Town House.

fig. 55. Tree-lined Muthill Road, Crieff, is the peaceful setting for this scene showing a Swift Cyclecar (TS 985). Cyclecars achieved a peak of popularity in the years leading up to the first war due mainly to their simplicity combined with low initial cost and subsequent low running cost.

fig. 56. A most utilitarian looking vehicle was this small Metz with Argyllshire number SB 888, dating it as early post First World War. This marque was imported from the U.S.A. where the cars were built in Waltham, Massachussets.

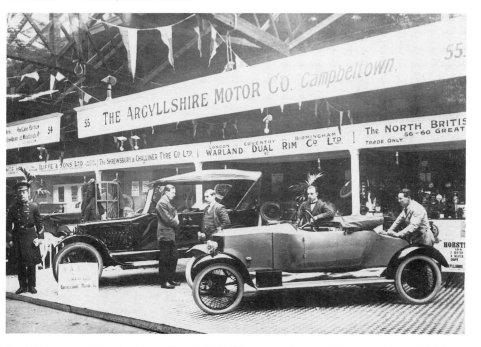

fig. 57. A scene within the original Kelvin Hall, Glasgow during one of the motor shows held there in the early 1920s. Stand 55 featured the Argyllshire Motor Co. of Campbeltown who were agents for both cars shown. On the left is a Saxon which despite its name was imported from Detroit and on the right an English Horstmann, built in Bath. Neither achieved much popularity in Scotland. *35*

fig. 58. Close inspection of this mid 1920s scene of the Sandgate in Ayr reveals a liveried chauffeur assisting a lady into a rather splendid Renault limousine of 1925, locally registered SD 8771. The cars parked in the right foreground appear to be a Sheffield-Simplex with a Sunbeam in front.

fig. 59. Heading towards Laggan Bridge from Spean Bridge on the Newtonmore road as it skirts the north shore of Loch Laggan. GB 4376 is a Buick of 1923, one of the many popular American imports of that period. Note the road surface which was then unmetalled.

fig. 60. A fine foursome at the Kirkmichael Hotel, Perthshire about 1924. From the left are a pre First World War G.W.K. Cyclecar, an Austin 20 saloon, a primitive looking Arrol Johnston 12 dating from the turn of the century with a six seat dogcart type body and finally a 15.9 H.P. Argyll cabriolet of the early 1920s.

fig. 61. The Bonnygate, Cupar, Fife in the mid 1920s with SP 9996 on the right, a Bean 4 seat open tourer. On the left, outside Leitch's cycle agency and garage is SP 2245, a much older pre-Great War open tourer, possibly a Hupmobile.

37

Winter Weather

fig. 62. A sleeve-valve Argyll 25/50 saloon cautiously makes its way down the flooded Loch Lomondside road between Luss and Balloch during severe weather conditions in December 1912. Its registration, appropriate for an Argyll was SB 142. In fact many Argylls not native to the county were purposefully registered with SB numbers — similarly we find many Vauxhalls were registered in Lanarkshire with V numbers.

fig. 63. 'Archiestown in Winter' is the caption on this picture post-card of the 1930s. The council workmen shovel the way clear for a little Austin 7 with its radiator well muffed to keep out the cold. This Morayshire village lies on a B road on the north side of Strathspey between Grantown and Rothes.

The People's Car

Before car ownership became as widespread as it is now, people relied much more on the bus for their travel. The following views show an interesting selection of early charabancs and motorbuses.

fig. 64. A damp day in Banff and the brollies are up as this Argus motorbus splashes along Bridge Street on the local route to Macduff operated by Horne's motor service around 1908. BK 425 came second hand from Portsmouth and there were few other examples of this German built chassis in Scotland.

fig. 65. As early as 1898, pioneer motorist and motor manufacturer John Stirling of Hamilton was operating Daimler wagonettes assembled and bodied in his own workshops. These ran in various coastal resorts including this one in Ayr which linked Prestwick, Ayr and Burns' Monument. Note the solid tyres, chain drive and tiller steering.

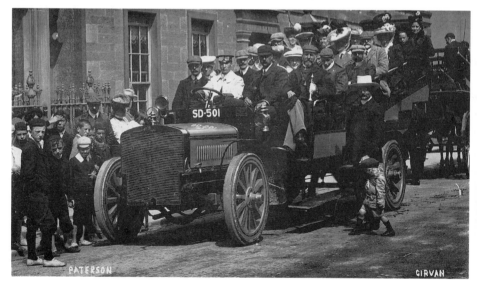

fig. 66. Also in Ayrshire we see a splendid Sheffield built Durham Churchill charabanc outside Thomas Lees' Kings Arms Hotel in Girvan in 1906. Lees operated horse drawn charabancs on a circular tour to Ballantrae returning by Colmonell and SD 501 was his first venture into the new world of motors. The guard, no doubt redundant from his horse drawn brake still holds his horn and what a fine array of headgear! Note the tiered seating to allow the passengers unrestricted views.

fig. 67. Among Scotland's pioneer motorists was E. J. Robertson-Grant of the Highland Park Distillery, Kirkwall, Orkney. He is seen here resplendent in a white suit at the wheel of S 486, the first motorbus to come to those Northern Isles. This was a 1905 Stirling built at Granton, which was one of two identical vehicles in the Orkney Motor Express fleet operated between Kirkwall and Stromness by a syndicate of local businessmen headed by Robertson-Grant. Amusingly, this route reverted to horse-drawn coaches around 1909 because of the unreliability of these motor-buses!

fig. 68. A view taken in 1907 on Rosemount Viaduct, Aberdeen, showing His Majesty's Theatre and the Wallace Statue. The motor vehicles are both buses owned by the Great North of Scotland Railway. SA 311, parked outside Schoolhill Station, was a primitive double-deck Milnes-Daimler with open top bodywork built by the G.N.S.R. themselves at their Inverurie workshops. It is about to depart for Newburgh.

fig. 69. When the motorcar was still in its infancy, motorbuses were even more of a phenomenon. Whole villages would turn out to stare in awe as they passed. An example is this scene in Waterton — Dunecht on the Aberdeen to Alford road when the arrival in 1907 of this Milnes-Daimler double decker (SA 312) owned by the Great North of Scotland Railway Co. caused quite a crowd outside the village post-office.

fig. 70. The massive radiator on XS 68 was fitted to an Arrol-Johnston charabanc owned by the North British Railway. It operated a service from 1905 until 1910 between North Berwick, Dirleton, Gullane and Aberlady and as may be expected in this area, was mainly used by golfers. Throughout Britain at this period the railway companies were among the first to introduce bus services from country districts, most of which connected with trains at the nearest railhead.

fig. 71. One of the most popular Scottish commercial chassis in Edwardian days was the Halley. Seen here is SX 275, a solid tyred, chain driven example delivered in 1912 to Jordan's Broxburn and Edinburgh Motor Service and optimistically named "The Seat of Comfort". After Halley's failure in 1935, their Yoker Factory was bought by Albion Motors.

43

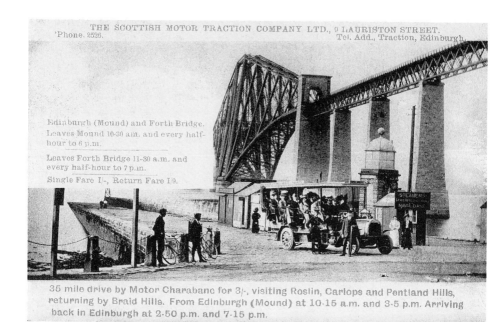

fig. 72.   An advertising card in circulation during the Edwardian infancy of the Scottish Motor Traction Co. Ltd. This shows one of their Maudslay charabancs at the Forth Bridge prior to departure back to the Mound in Edinburgh, which was the tours stance at that time. Note the fares charged at that period!

fig. 73. The celebrations for the Coronation of King George V in 1910 extended throughout the country. The S.M.T. Co. Ltd. of Edinburgh was then barely 5 years old but was to grow to become the parent of Scotland's largest bus organisation. This Maudslay double-decker was one of the original S.M.T. vehicles, delivered in early 1906 and is seen here operating between Edinburgh and Pumpherston.

44

fig. 74. The most popular home-produced commercial chassis in Scotland was undoubtedly the Albion. This 1921 example, fitted with a charabanc body was operated by Blair of the Trossachs Hotel who had progressed to the motor vehicle from 4 in hand horse-drawn coaches. Many passengers joined his Trossachs tours from trains arriving at Callander station. ES 2978 is seen here crossing the Brig O' Turk, spanning the Finglas Water.

fig. 75. The border village of Town Yetholm in 1927 on the morning of the annual bus trip to the seaside at Spittal near Berwick on Tweed. The charabancs belonged to Turnbull of Kelso and are of Maudslay, Leyland and Albion manufacture. The two boys in the foreground appear to be watching events rather wistfully. Perhaps their turn would come the following year.

fig. 76. When the Leyland Tiger was introduced in 1927 it revolutionised the operations of many bus companies throughout the land and was popular with passengers and drivers alike. Until this time some firms still ran antiquated lumbering solid tyred models. MS 8835 was a typical Tiger delivered in 1929 to Walter Alexander of Falkirk with bodywork built by the operator. It is seen on the long journey from Aberdeen to Glasgow above the coastal village of Gourdon, Kincardineshire.

fig. 77. Princes Street, Edinburgh in 1929 when this splendid Daimler luxury coach was new. It was owned by Thomson's Tours, who operated an Edinburgh to London service and also a considerable touring programme. The coachwork, which gives the vehicle the appearance of a huge private car, was built by the Hoyal Body Corporation of Weybridge, Surrey.

fig. 78. For a short time after the Road Traffic Act of 1930 came into force, a service of 7 seater limousines was operated between Glasgow and London, as a speedier alternative to the normal bus service. Seen at the top of Buchanan Street, Glasgow on an advertising promotion is GG 2575, a Detroit built Hudson Super 8 of 1931 with similar Hudson GE 9311 just visible behind.

fig. 80. David MacBrayne provided many rural bus services throughout Scotland's Western Highlands and Islands. Many of these were subsidised by the Post Office as they also carried mail. One such service linked the villages of Carrick Castle and Lochgoilhead with Arrochar and Tarbet station. Seen at Carrick Castle is a Bedford of 1952 with 20 seat body by Duple which incorporated a mail compartment at the back.

fig. 79. Gourock Pierhead, 1936. The line of parked cars is headed by YS 1436, a gleaming Humber 12 saloon of 1935 with the registration letters taken over by Glasgow from the burgh of Partick that year. Plenty motorbus interest too, with Leyland single deckers of Western S.M.T. including a new Cheetah heading for Largs and 6-wheel Tigers facing Glasgow. The Leyland double deckers belong to Greenock Motor Services, the one on the right being VS 1111, a Titan TDI delivered in 1929 for local routes in Gourock, Greenock and Port Glasgow. Just visible to the left are the masts and funnels of a Clyde steamer.

fig. 81. The general appearance of the Austin was similar to that of the Bedford. DST 358 was an Austin with 14 seat body by Scunthorpe Motors bought by MacLennan of Shieldaig in 1949 for his mail contract between that Ross-shire fishing village and the railhead at Strathcarron. It is seen here on the lonely road between Tornapress and Shieldaig. The MacLennan family have operated this **service continuously for over 70 years.**

49

Caravanning and Camping

Fig. 82. Although caravans were in use from the earliest days of motoring they were generally purpose-built 'one-offs'. Caravanettes as we know them today were also specially built. SN 1747 was a model T Ford owned by bus operators Alexander of Falkirk who had also built its caravan body. It was advertised in their tour booklet for 1925 (reproduced here) as available for hire to the public.

Alexanders' Motor Touring Caravan.

We have now added to our fleet of cars a CARAVAN, fully equipped with the necessary utensils for an ideal holiday. Those anticipating a holiday in the above should make enquiries for our terms at an early date as we are now booking.

For full particulars write, 'phone or call at

The Garage,
Brown Street,

266 Falkirk.   Camelon, Falkirk
or   W. Alexander & Sons Ltd.
Edward Street

95 Kilsyth   Kilsyth.

fig. 83. A mid 1920s camping scene at Aviemore, with Craigellachie Rock in the background. The Speyside resort was a popular centre even in those days when few would have foreseen the major developments to take place in and around the village. A Buick Roadster tows a caravan of the style produced by Eccles of Birmingham, who are reckoned to have built Britain's first production tourer caravans.

fig. 84. A Carabus? The similarity to a double decker bus is perhaps not surprising as this luxurious Bedford caravan of the early 1930s was built and owned by charabanc and cinema entrepreneur Peter Crerar of Crieff. It had beds for six, fitted kitchen, bathroom and even a bar, but was not for public hire.

fig. 85. This mid 1950s view shows a Bedford Dormobile on board the Kylesku ferry *Mamore* which made the crossing over Loch Cairnbawn in Sutherland (compare with fig. 109). Since 1984 the new Kylesku Bridge has allowed traffic easier access to the far north, as summer bottlenecks were prevalent in the days of the ferry.

Picnics by Car

fig. 86. Adam Purves, motor hirer of Galashiels owned this Selkirkshire registered Argyll LS 117. On this occasion it was hired to local photographer Clapperton of Galashiels for a picnic outing with his family to St Mary's Loch. Clapperton sold this view locally as a picture post-card.

fig. 87. A pre-1914 Glasgow registered Rolls-Royce Silver Ghost has brought these two couples for a picnic by the shores of Loch Tay sometime in the early 1920s. The Rolls-Royce of course is said to be the best car in the world. The Silver Ghost was certainly the model which initiated that fine reputation and had a lengthy production run from 1906 until 1925.

fig. 88. The occupants of these solid looking automobiles were driving all the way from Bothwell in Lanarkshire to the South of England. This was probably one of several *al fresco* roadside picnics enjoyed en route. The cars were AS 501, appropriately an Armstrong-Siddeley 30 H.P. model of about 1921 and G 2619, an older Deasy tourer, dating from pre–1st War days.

fig. 89. Picnics on the beach at Seamill, Ayrshire, looking towards the hills of Arran across the Firth of Clyde. It must surely have been a fine summer day judging by the number of parked cars which include SN 2984, which appears to be a Morris Cowley two seat tourer of 1925 with open dickey and next to it a new Morris 8. The year of this photo was 1935.

Morris Motors

fig. 90. The notice at some unidentified seaside resort reads 'I might be yours for sixpence. Try your luck.' Not particularly dignified, perhaps, but the sturdy Bullnose Morris Cowley had no pretensions of grandeur. It was however a popular and reliable workhorse and is now a firm favourite amongst vintage car enthusiasts. (see fig. 166)

fig. 91. The larger Morris Oxford Bullnose had a 13.9 H.P. engine as compared with the Cowley's 11.9. Seen here at Southerness lighthouse on the Solway Firth is SM 5232, a Dumfries registered Oxford of 1925. The term 'Bullnose' refers of course to the distinctive radiator used on these models.

fig. 92. Another example of a mid 1920s Morris Oxford Bullnose (this time with hood raised) seen in company with a 14 seat Clyde bus of 1921. The location is the small garage owned by Hamilton Jackson in the Lanarkshire village of Auchenheath, where he owned the local bus service connecting Lanark, Lesmahagow and Strathaven. The Clyde commercial vehicle chassis were built by Mackay and Jardine of Wishaw until the late 1920s , but no private cars were manufactured.

fig. 93. Alex. Cowe, erstwhile proprietor of the MacDonald Arms Hotel, Tobermory, on the Isle of Mull is seen here in 1929 with two of his hiring fleet. The car on the left is a Studebaker, while on the right is ST 4729, a 14 seat Morris Commercial charabanc of 1927 which operated day tours around the island. This scene is at Tom a Vullin.

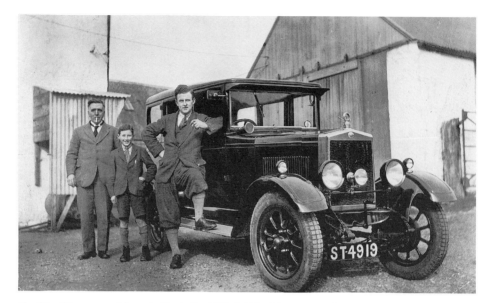

fig. 94. Three proud faces indicate that ST 4919 had been recently purchased by Mr. Cameron of the Harris Hotel. Tarbert, Isle of Harris when this view was taken in 1928. It was a Morris Oxford Flatnose mainly for use as a hire car. The 'Flatnose' was introduced for the 1927 season to replace the 'Bullnose' model.

fig. 95. A splendid M.G. 14/28 of around 1927 poses in the Fife coast fishing village of Crail. The 4 seat open tourer had an engine-turned patterned, (or curled according to a contemporary catalogue) aluminium body.

fig. 96. Lord Nuffield's answer to the baby Austin 7 was the Morris Minor, introduced in 1929. JO 2287 is an Oxford registered Minor of 1931 with 2 seat open tourer body. In that year Morris reduced the price of this model to £100 which was the first new British car to be sold at such a sum. This peaceful scene was in Court Street, Haddington, East Lothian.

fig. 97. In June 1933 the main Inverness — Fort William road was upgraded along the north side of Loch Ness. On the extreme left of this view is William Tawse, the Aberdeen contractor for the scheme and the superb automobile is GU 6487, a Belgian Minerva, registered in London.

Cars and Ferries

Scotland's geography of wide firths and, on the west coast, numerous offshore islands and sea lochs making long inroads into the coastline, made ferry crossings an important connecting link with the road system.

fig. 98. An Edwardian scene showing a Daimler perched somewhat precariously across the Ballachulish Ferry which was powered only by oars in those days. Those who remember the swift current encountered when crossing the mouth of Loch Leven will appreciate that rowing a laden boat must have been no mean feat.

fig. 99. Ballachulish Ferry again, but in 1931 when a motor vessel was in use. It is seen at North Ballachulish carrying an Austin 16 saloon, while a group of hikers wait to cross to the Appin shore over a very placid Loch Leven. This ferry was replaced in 1975 by a bridge, thus removing the sometimes long frustrating delays often encountered in summer.

fig. 100. Only a few miles north from the Ballachulish crossing, the Corran Ferry plies across the Corran Narrows of Loch Linnhe to Ardgour from where the single track road leads towards the Ardnamurchan peninsula. This mid 1930s scene shows the ferry arriving from Ardgour with an Austin 16 on board. This example differs from that in the last view by virtue of its Tickford cabriolet body with hood rolled down fully on this occasion.

fig. 101. We take a long drive up the west coast to our next ferry. This is the summer only crossing to Kylerhea on the Isle of Skye over the Sound of Sleat from Glenelg on the west coast of Inverness-shire. This photograph dates from 1936 and shows a Wolseley 14 arriving at the mainland shore while waiting to board are a model Y Ford, an Austin 12 and a B.S.A. three-wheeler, each having negotiated the Mam Ratagan hill road from Shiel Bridge.

Speed Bonny Boat . . .

fig. 102. The ferry between Kyle of Lochalsh in Wester Ross and Kyleakin on the Isle of Skye sails all the year round in contrast to the summer only operation at Kylerhea. This scene at Kyle in the late 1920s shows a queue of cars waiting for the right state of the tide to make the crossing to Skye. Nearest the camera is GE 2771, a Ford A Tudor of 1928 with TS 4728, a Morris Cowley tourer of 1925 in front.

fig. 103. At the Kyleakin side about 1933. On board is a Riley, while two small buses bring passengers and mail from north and south Skye. These are an Albion of the Skye Transport Co. which has travelled down from Portree (note the luggage being unloaded from the roof) and a Morris Commercial owned by MacLean and MacDonald of Ardvasar which has arrived from Sleat.

fig. 104. 'Over the sea to Skye' in 1952. The ferry arrives at Kyle from Kyleakin with a Fordson van and a Wolseley while waiting to cross to the Misty Isle are MUV 100, a new Austin A40 Devon of 1952 and a Jowett Javelin with its unmistakable sloping back. DST 695 was a 1950 model.

60

fig. 105. One of several west coast ferries which are now but a memory. Before the mouth of Loch Long in Wester Ross was spanned by a bridge, one had to use the Aird Ferry when travelling to Kyle of Lochalsh. It is seen here on the Ardelve side having loaded ST 393, an Inverness-shire registered Austin of 1910. The village of Dornie is visible on the opposite shore.

fig. 106. Prior to the completion of the road around the head of Loch Carron, motor traffic for the far north crossed the loch by Strome Ferry. Leaving the ferry is a 1949 Commer Commando coach in the fleet of Lawson's of Kirkintilloch, who enjoyed a good reputation for their Highland Tours or Land Cruises as they were known. The coachwork was by Scottish Aviation who built a considerable number of bus bodies at their Prestwick Airport premises in the late 1940s and early 1950s.

61

fig. 107. As recently as 1984 the well known chain ferry across the Clyde between Renfrew and Yoker was replaced by a passenger only vessel. This 1936 view at the Renfrew side shows the old ferry as many will still remember. A Paisley registered Morris Cowley Flatnose with open tourer body leaves ahead of US 7075, a Morris 10/4.

fig. 108. Down river from Renfrew, the similar Erskine chain ferry plied back and forward to Old Kilpatrick. This view from the late 1940s shows BAG 516, an AEC Regal coach owned by Dodds of Troon, leaving at the Erskine side to head home after a day tour to Oban. This ferry became redundant in 1971 when the Erskine bridge was opened.

fig. 109. A sea-loch crossing replaced by a bridge as lately as 1984 was over Loch Cairnbawn in Sutherland. Here we see the Kylesku Ferry in the mid 1920s, with a Morris Cowley four seat open tourer on board. At that time a charge was made for the crossing but later the county council took over operation and introduced free passage.

fig. 110. East coast ferries were less numerous, the most important being those across the Forth and Tay estuaries. This scene shows a stormy day at North Queensferry in the early 1950s as SB 6722, an immediate post-war Vauxhall 14 H.P. J type drives through the spray to board. The demise of this crossing followed on completion of the Forth Road Bridge in 1963.

Trains and Boats and Planes...

fig. 111. Probably taken in Balloch when both railway engine and motor car were new in 1906. The Argyll GD 16 (trade plates) appears diminutive in comparison with the Caledonian Railway locomotive no 919. Both were all-Scottish products, the Argyll built at the ornate factory in nearby Alexandria and the engine at St. Rollox works in Glasgow.

fig. 112. Port Ellen on the Isle of Islay, on Glasgow Fair Saturday 1926. The pier is thronged with a variety of motor vehicles to meet the laden *Pioneer* as she arrives from West Loch Tarbert. In the foreground are HS 3995 a new Morris Cowley Bullnose and SB 1637, a 1921 model T Ford charabanc owned by McIntyre's Machrie Hotel and named *Maid of Islay*.

fig. 113. Whiting Bay on the Isle of Arran is no longer a port of call for Clyde passenger ferries; in fact the pier itself no longer exists. However, when this scene was taken in the late 1940s it was a hive of activity at steamer time. A long line of pre-war taxis awaits custom, as do the wartime utility Bedford buses, owned by Gordon Brothers of Lamlash. These Spartan vehicles with their slatted wooden seats certainly left their passengers with an impression of Arran!

fig. 114. A Ford V8 shooting brake new in 1936 and used for passengers between Lerwick and Shetland airport at Sumburgh connecting with Allied Airways flights to and from the Scottish mainland. AV 8740 is seen alongside a De Havilland D.H. 84 Dragon.

...and Trams

fig. 115. Murraygate, Dundee has always been a popular shopping street. It would appear that the chauffeur in splendid white uniform and peaked cap is waiting the return of a lady gone to make purchases. His taxi is TS 726, a Napier of 1910, with Corporation tramcar No 13 approaching. A length of tram track can still be seen in the pedestrianised Murraygate today.

fig. 116. The last tram ran in Scotland in Glasgow in 1962, but formerly all the Scottish cities and some of the larger towns had tramway systems. Streets with tram lines were inevitably laid with granite setts or cobbles, necessitating extra care on the part of the motorist. In this mid 1950s scene at Paisley Cross, the Morris Oxford appears almost to be gnashing its teeth as it drives between Glasgow Corporation Coronation type tramcars and a Foden double decker of Smith's bus service, Barrhead.

fig. 117. Edinburgh Castle looks down over Princes Street in tramway days (the last one ran here in 1956). EJA 733, a Stockport registered Triumph Mayflower of 1951 heads east along Scotland's famous thoroughfare between Corporation tram and a Guy Arab 'decker of the municipal bus fleet. By summer 1955 when this view was taken the trams were being replaced by new Leyland Titan buses, also visible in this scene.

Three Sevens plus a Ten

fig. 118. A rear view of a baby Austin 7 seen in Glenapp driving north towards Ballantrae. Glenapp is where the main A77 coast road from Stranraer cuts inland north of Cairnryan. This seven carried the Motherwell and Wishaw registration GM 1284, new in 1928.

fig. 119. The old school at Broadford, Isle of Skye, and RG 2675, an Aberdeen registered Austin 7 of 1932 with its owner. The well loved baby Austin had been introduced in 1922 and production continued for sixteen years during which time it effectively squashed all competition from the remaining cyclecar manufacturers.

fig. 120. An advert of the mid 1930s featuring the Austin 7.

fig. 121. WS 9181, an Austin 10 of 1936 pauses at the Half-Way House Restaurant and Filling Station near Invermoriston on the main Inverness-Fort William road along the north shore of Loch Ness. The 10 had four doors as opposed to the 7 which had only two.

fig. 122. Inside a typical coachbuilder's premises around 1930. The body shop in question was owned by Jackson of Dunfermline who dealt with both private and commercial work. Among the vehicles under repair are FG 3689, a Vulcan bus of 1928 owned by Clark of Glencraig with Crossley and Studebaker (FG 5587) saloon cars behind.

fig. 123. Lonely Aultguish Hotel, on the road between Garve and Ullapool is the setting for this wintry scene about 1934.The small Chevrolet lorry on the left has snow chains fitted to the rear wheels but the occupants of the two cars seem quite unconcerned about the road conditions. The leading car is a Rover, while to the right is a model A Ford van. Both Chevrolet and Ford date from 1931,the British built Chev. being an example of one of the last produced at Luton before the Bedford was introduced.

70

fig. 124. A fine line-up of quality cars outside Holyrood Palace in Edinburgh. The hire cars are Sunbeams, flanked at both ends by police cars from the City of Edinburgh Force. Nearest the camera, SC 9022 is a Morris Isis of 1930, with POLICE on the headlamps, while at the far end is an Austin 20, neither of which were the swiftest of cars for a Flying Squad.

fig. 125. Throughout the 1920s and 1930s the Police Force grew progressively more mobile. This was the fleet of Renfrew and Bute Constabulary vehicles seen in 1931 outside Blythswood House, Renfrew (now demolished). Along with the Sunbeam and B.S.A. motor cycles are HS 5582, a 1929 Morris Cowley Flatnose; HS 6222, a 1931 Armstrong Siddeley and HS 6004, a 1930 Standard. One assumes that the policy of this force was to purchase one new car per year at this period.

'Fordors', 'Tudors' and a 'Y'

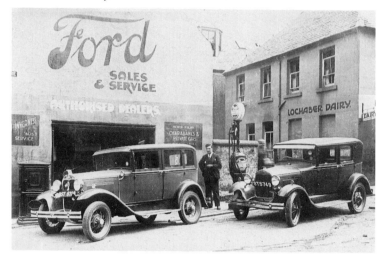

fig. 126. A MacIntyre & Sons were the Ford agents in Fort William. Outside their premises in Monzie Square are two model A Fords of the Fordor type, as opposed to the Tudor which had only two doors. These were both locally registered ST 6116 and ST 5749 of 1930 and 1929 respectively. MacIntyre also operated the bus service from Fort William to Inverness as may be seen from their adverts on the wall.

fig. 127. Bridge of Cally, Perthshire lies at the junction of the roads from Braemar and from Pitlochry to Blairgowrie, thus the petrol pumps at the local hotel were in regular demand. Seen here in the mid 1930s is a B.S.A. motor cycle (GS160) filling up (note the sign 1/4d. per gallon) while parked outside the hotel are GS 843, a 1929 Ford A Tudor and an Austin 10 saloon of around 1934.

fig. 128. A Ford model A Tudor saloon of the early 1930s at the Parkhill Hotel, Durness, in the far north-west corner of Scotland. This was the type of car which replaced the long-lived model T in 1927.

fig. 129. Loch Lomondside and a powdering of snow on the Ben in this 1934 scene between Luss and Inverbeg. A new 8 H.P. Y type Ford sits by the roadside. The following year the price of this two door saloon was reduced from £120 to £100 becoming the first closed car in the U.K. to be sold at this price.

fig. 130. In the lee of Ben More at Crianlarich,Perthshire, this atmospheric scene in 1938 shows GE 8250, a Singer Junior of 1930 with its kilted driver seeking advice from the A.A. patrolman on his B.S.A. motor cycle combination. Meanwhile a train for Fort William hauled by two Glen Class locos of the L.N.E.R. steams across the bridge out of Crianlarich station.

fig. 131. Main Street, Rutherglen, seen from the Cross in 1939 with two late 1920s Morris Cowley Flatnose saloons followed by a Morris 10/4, while two open staircase Leyland Titans belonging to Central S.M.T. head for the city.

fig. 132. A 1933 Armstrong-Siddeley 20 H.P., complete with the famous sphinx mascot on the radiator, pauses at the border sign post at Carter Bar on the A 68 road over the Cheviots. The occupants were probably heading home for the south of England as NJ 1961 was registered in East Sussex.

fig. 133. A six cylinder Morris of 1934 poses beside Queen Mary's Tree on the Old Dalkeith Road at Little France on the southern outskirts of Edinburgh. Mary Queen of Scots is reputed to have named the village and planted the tree, since gone. Note the semaphore trafficator on the car, signalling right.

fig. 134. The fluted bonnet and griffin radiator mascot show GD 7802 unmistakably as one of the Vauxhall breed. This was a six cylinder sleeve-valve model of 1928, seen here in the mid 1930s dodging a cyclist in Glasgow's Bath Street approaching the Buchanan Street junction, with Skerry's College in the background.

fig. 135. A 6 cylinder American Oakland saloon of around 1930 seen touring at the Brig O' Feugh near Banchory, Kincardineshire in 1935, while the ladies admire the view. The registration number of this car is particularly interesting as US 391 was issued by the old Burgh of Govan. US numbers had only reached 529 before the City of Glasgow took over in 1933.

fig. 136. A 1936 view showing Airdrie Cross and Stirling Street with YJ 3580, a Ford Y type and HS 9056 a Morris 8, both new in that year. An Albion bus owned by Irvine of Glenmavis sets down passengers at the stop behind the cars, while to the left is a Fiat taxi of the mid 1920s.

A City Street

fig. 137. (Top, opposite.) Looking up Buchanan Street from St. Enoch Square during the reign of King Edward VII. The only motor vehicle in sight amongst all the horse-drawn traffic is a chauffeur driven Deasy car crossing Argyle Street junction, while an open balcony Corporation tramcar may be seen passing Samuel's corner. There may not have been the fumes from motor vehicle exhausts in those early days but with so many horses other odours must have been equally obnoxious.

fig. 138. (Below, opposite) Buchanan Street in 1926. Already motor vehicles were causing sufficient congestion to warrant surveillance from mounted traffic police. This view outside Miss Cranston's tearooms shows a French built Latil charabanc with the fleet name *Mac* while behind is GB 3787, a 20 H.P. Rolls Royce of the early 1920s and a model T Ford taxi.

fig. 139. Buchanan Street at its junction with St. Vincent Place in 1935 when the Corporation Albion Venturer bus was new. Fleet number 6 (YS 2006) had bodywork by Cowieson of St. Rollox, who built much of the pre-war municipal bus fleet. It was one of the first batch of buses with diesel engines (Gardners) delivered to the Corporation. Heading up the street is a Morris Oxford 6 fabric saloon of about 1932. The mid 1930s fashions are equally noteworthy!

79

fig. 140. Nowadays, apart from the bus stance much of St. Enoch Square and Buchanan Street is a pedestrian precinct. This makes it all the more appropriate to recall the days when street and square were filled with motor traffic. Here we see St. Enoch Square, looking towards Buchanan Street in the mid 1950s with the old St. Enoch Railway Station on the right. A typical selection of motor vehicles of the period is visible, the more prominent ones being a 1954 Rover (bottom right)

with a Guy Wolf pantechnicon behind. Coaches of Lowland Motorways are parked outside the air terminal and in the centre of the square from where they shuttled to and from Renfrew Airport. These included A.E.C. Regals, a Bedford and an Albion, while a Glasgow Corporation double deck Daimler leaves its stance for Croftfoot on service 5. Among the other makes of cars apart from the Austin FX3 taxicabs are Vauxhall, Humber, Morris, Hillman and Ford. The more you look, the more you find.

fig. 141. The use of a commercial vehicle chassis as the base for a shooting brake body was not uncommon, but naturally a more expensive purchase than a private car. One such example was this short wheelbase Albion Victor delivered to Lord Glentanar of Aboyne, Aberdeenshire in 1935. It was registered in the county as AV 7569 and is seen with a group of keepers in the hills on Glentanar estate.

fig. 142. (Top opposite) A view on the spectacular Bealach na Ba or the Pass of the Cattle on the mountain road between Tornapress and Applecross, Wester Ross. Climbing the pass (which reaches 2,054 ft with a 1 in 4 gradient) during a rally organised by the R.S.A.C. is CPF 211, a Surrey registered Singer Le Mans of 1935. As may be seen the road was rough and narrow at that time, and even now must be treated with respect.

fig. 143. (Below, opposite) King Street, Kilmarnock in 1936 with VD 6451, a new Riley Kestrel of rather sporty appearance passing a Leyland Cub delivery lorry of 1932. This section of the street has now a one-way traffic system.

fig. 144. Looking west along Fort William High Street from the West Highland Museum at the corner of Cameron Square. This view dates from 1936 and shows the almost inevitable model Y Ford parked outside the Playhouse cinema, while driving towards the camera is a Ford V-8.

fig. 145. A schoolgirl waits to cross Glasgow Road from the corner of Church Street, Blantyre in 1937. Two of the ubiquitous 8 H.P. model Y Fords are evident, with a Morris 8 in the centre. In the background, a Central S.M.T. Leyland Titan heads towards Hamilton.

fig. 146. A typical Ford advertisement of the mid 1930s featuring cars seen in the preceding views.   *85*

fig. 147. Framed in an archway at Stirling Castle is AMO 342, a 2 litre M.G. saloon registered in Berkshire in 1937. M.G. stood for Morris Garages, initials which have always been synonymous with lively sports cars.

fig. 148. The village of Innellan, Argyll, with CGA 742 a solid looking Rover 12 saloon of 1938 parked outside the post office.

fig. 149. Petrol had gone up by a penny to 1/5d (see fig. 127.) by the time this photo was taken at the pumps outside the Ochil Tea Rooms at Muckhart, Perthshire in 1939. About to fill up with *Redline* is FXE 202, a London registered Hillman Minx new that year. The occupants have opened the sunshine roof to enjoy the fine day.

fig. 150. Touring in 1939 before the dark days of wartime introduced all their various restrictions on private motoring. On the rough road at Camus na Croise, above Loch Linnhe on its Morven shore we see SS 3100, a 1930 Buick probably enjoying its last days of freedom. The Union Jack and G.B. plate suggest that this car had travelled outwith Britain.

Forties and Fifties

fig. 151. An early post-war view of Lochwinnoch Road at Kilmacolm Cross, Renfrewshire, with an S.S. Jaguar of 1939. BHS 360 was a 2½ litre model, with drophead coupé coachwork. Behind it is a wartime Austin K2 van of Chipperfields Circus which was probably an ex W.D. vehicle.

fig. 152. The fish market at Macduff, Banffshire, generates a crowd of eager spectators in early post-war days, but more interesting to us is the line of vehicles headed by SE 4091, a locally registered Dodge of 1935 fitted with a pick-up body.

fig. 153. The Devil's Elbow on the Blairgowrie — Braemar road was well-known in automobile circles but it too is now but a motoring memory. It was particularly notorious in the early days of motoring with its double bends and gradients reaching 1 in 5. This view taken just after the last war shows CSA 155, an Albion in the fleet of Jas. Sutherland, Peterhead, negotiating the Elbow followed by GM 2929, a 1937 14/6 Vauxhall and HH 7713, a 1934 Austin 12.

fig. 154. A 1949 photograph showing a number of interesting vehicles parked outside the railway station at Ballater on Deeside. Nearest the camera is a Hillman of the mid 1930s, while to the right is a post-war Ford Prefect fitted uncharacteristically with a wooden shooting-brake body. In the background, Alexander's service bus from Aberdeen to Braemar (a pre-war Leyland Tiger) waits departure time.

fig. 155. The towns in the northern Isles of Orkney and Shetland all have narrow streets, many without pavements.Extra care is thus required on the part of both motorist and pedestrian, as may be seen in this late 1940s view of Stromness with BS 2291 an Orkney registered Austin 10, new in 1946.

fig. 156. Dingwall High Street in 1950, with Morrises in the majority. In the foreground is CLM 845 which was by then an elderly Morris 8 of 1935, with HSG 483, a brand new split-windscreen Minor of 1950 driving up the street towards a J type van which can be seen parked on the right.

90

fig. 157. Looking from the pierhead up the main street in Largs, Ayrshire in 1949. Prominent is FRF 433 a 3½ litre S.S. Jaguar of 1937 with Staffordshire registration, while a Clyde Coast Services double decker leaves for Saltcoats. Jaguar only became a manufacturer's name from 1945, having previously been given only to certain S.S. models, as in this example. S.S. Cars Ltd. of Coventry became Jaguar Cars Ltd. in that year. On the right is a Morris 10.

fig. 158. The Common Green, Strathaven, Lanarkshire, on a summer day in 1951. In the foreground is HGA 188, a 1949 Sunbeam-Talbot followed by BGD 547, a 1937 Ford 10. Alongside is FGE 183, a post war Ford Prefect of 1947 while in the background, two Leyland Titans of Central S.M.T. wait at the bus stance.

fig. 159. East High Street, Forfar, in the early 1950s with a variety of motoring interest including DHS 275 a 1947 Standard 8 parked in the foreground with FFG 306 an immediate post-war Ford Anglia behind. VMF 394, an Austin A 70 of 1950 drives towards the camera.

fig. 160. The main street (Chalmers Street) in Ardrishaig has undergone considerable changes since the time of this early 1950s scene. SB 9031, a 1952 Vauxhall Velox, has drawn up at the erstwhile Anchor Hotel pumps, while behind it can be seen SB 8602, an Austin Somerset of 1951. Most of the buildings on the right have now disappeared.

fig. 161. The Edinburgh — Lauder road south of Soutra Hill with a decorated gypsy van from Londonderry, Northern Ireland on its way to St. Boswell's Fair in 1952. Climbing towards Soutra is SY 9969, an Austin A 40 pick-up of 1951, while the elderly Rolls-Royce parked in the lay-by is OG 8143 of 1930.

fig. 162. Paisley in the early 1950s. A Johnstone bound Daimler recently acquired from Young's Bus Service by Western S.M.T. sets down passengers at the bus stop at the corner of New Street, while Morris, Ford, Austin, Opel and Standard cars can be seen on the cobbled High Street, with a Glasgow tramcar in the distance.

fig. 163. A scene at Kyleakin on the Isle of Skye during the summer of 1956. Heading the ferry queue at the top of the slip is Ayrshire registered JSD 655, a new Hillman Minx which no doubt had conveyed its owners on holiday to Eilan Sgiatheanach. Nowadays the much larger ferries making the crossing to the mainland have reduced traffic delays to a minimum.

fig. 164. Inverness towards the end of the 1950s. A wide variety of cars are parked in Union Street towards the Station Hotel in the distance. Outside Melven's bookshop is OSM 343 a Dumfries registered 1953 Morris Oxford with an interesting pre-war American Chrysler behind. Continuing along the line we see TSM 552 a 1956 Jaguar while on the left is HST 640 a locally registered Austin A 50 of 1955.

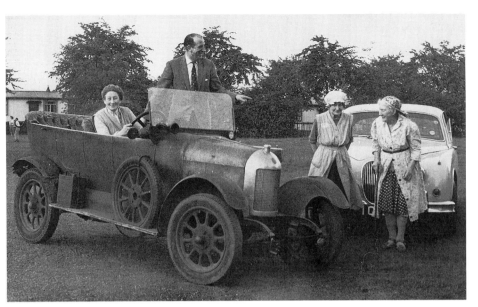

fig. 165. & fig. 166. Restoration of vintage cars is a most satisfying task. The author was fortunate to obtain this Morris Cowley 'Bullnose' tourer in the mid 1960s when the Gilchrist sisters moved from their farm in Renfrew due to housing development. In the upper view, show business personality Archie McCulloch visits the sisters at Newmains Farm to see the car which they had run continuously since 1922. The lower picture shows the Bullnose (registered V 9969) as it is today. Although old cars become harder to find as the years progress, it is still surprising what may be tucked away in some forgotten corner just waiting to be restored to its former glory.

Acknowledgments

Most of the illustrations are from my own collection, gathered over many years from so many sources that it is impossible to remember them all. Suffice to record my grateful thanks to all the motorists, many of them pioneers in their own right who have helped me, albeit unwittingly, in the compilation of *Motoring Memories*.

The following deserve special mention for granting permission to use views from their collections:–

NB Traction Group, Dundee:	**figs. 18, 61, 65, 95, 117.**
J. Cummings, London:	**fig. 70.**
Scotsman Publications, Edinburgh:	**fig. 110.**
J. Thomson, Glasgow:	**fig. 106**
C. P. Stewart, Hamilton:	**fig. 38.**
I. Coonie, Paisley:	**fig. 116.**
George Oliver, Glasgow:	**figs. 59, 83, 91, 97, 100, 124, 132, 133, 147, 150, 161.**
George Waugh, Glasgow:	**figs. 17, 26, 32, 33, 50, 51, 57, 85, 87, 96, 157, 159, 163, 164.**

I would also like to express my gratitude to Jonathan Lord and the staff of the Royal Scottish Automobile Club, Glasgow; Brian Lambie of the Biggar Museum Trust; Larry McDougall of Glasgow Transport Museum; Jim Savage of Leith and Jim Wardlaw of Kilmarnock for their help with vehicle identification, and to Isaac McCaig of Campsie Glen for the artwork on the front cover (based on the Peugeot in **fig. 9**). The back cover, which features a Morgan Super Sports tri-car taking part in a hill climb comes from a children's annual of the early 1930s with additions by Ian Clydesdale Graphics of Renfrew.

Hope you enjoyed the book. Watch out for 'More Motoring Memories.'